ELECTRIC SOUL

Poetry

Journey into an electric world with electric souls.
Imagination and meaning.
Words with an electric charge.
Soul poems from one electric soul to another…

For the ones who sing with the electricity in their soul...

that spark of electricity
in your soul
that makes you, you

she's the whole circuit board
electricity lives in her soul

you were grasping at it before
but now you hold the flesh of the universe
the cosmic dust in your gentle hands
and you're creating such sweet melodies

the music
of the world
thrums through
every fibre
and she shines
with the electric light
in her soul

golden light of
the bleeding sun
warms my heart
before the stars shine
with starlight fire

the night has many wonders
curious lights that glisten in the sky
the day transforms
like a florescent butterfly
into the night of all
beautiful possibilities
and reckless young minds

living forever is easy
but can you live with
the person you've become

that night
by the look in your eyes
I could see all the electricity
stirring in your soul

she told me her soul poems
and I knew then
she was sharing some
of her electric light
with me
under the glow
of those midnight stars

she's become
a master at the
art of poetry

she's got many talents
in her repertoire
storytelling maestro
mover of imagination
electricity conductor

a water dancer
electric blue eyes
how skilfully
you move
through this game
we call life

creative soul
go to the valley
in your mind
where none
have gone before
where you built
a garden of your desires
and your heart,
a fortress of
midnight music
the beautiful sound
of your soul

the best thing about imagination
is making real what you see in your mind

electric nights
with you
the music
and eternity

I could live
off the feeling
that electronic music
gives me

a gathering of souls
to hear the sound waves
pulsate in our veins
and ignite in our hearts
under the electric sky
to feel more than alive

she speaks the language of the universe
hums the music of the stars
and understands the story of the cosmos

she's forging her own path
with fingers dipped in forbidden paint

she's learning
that the beat
and the rhythm
of the world
is sometimes
in sync with
her own heart
and sometimes
hers is different
like we are the
whole universe
in a body
but with unique
personal antennas

she has the mindset of a warrior
and treads carefully in the realm of her mind

she knows she has what it takes
she'll find the will inside her to bloom

creativity is hearing
your soul whispers
and acting on them

celestial blue stars
coated in my courage
and built in my heart

when we'd run
through dandelion fields
with wild hair and fireflies
and watch the night fox
as he gazed at the stars
in the midnight sky
and talk of tales
that made us wonder
because we thought
that's how the world was
built on stories and
destiny and the magic
in a little girl's heart
maybe the world is like that,
her world is

an electric girl
with an electric soul

you've gained nothing
if you've lost your soul

coming home to yourself
feels like stars igniting
and bursting in your veins

will you write about me in your story?

resurgence in the blooming of your heart

carnival colours
of your painted heart
an artist of storytelling
at candlelight hour
you danced all night
in the dreams
you dipped so beautifully
in the light of your soul

life's mysterious game
you played the design
only to loop and find yourself

she's beautifully broken
in all the tender places
that's how the glitter gets in

you have a gift girl
you can listen to a story
and understand
the hidden meaning
woven into the allegory
it's like you hear the words
in the electronic music
even when there are none

listen to the trees when you
walk alone in the woods
they have something to tell you

I've said things to you
I've only ever whispered to my soul

at night she'd walk along the river
and chat with the universe
inside her head,
kingdoms grow on clouds
of stardust and imagination

she danced with eternity
in the electric lights
like fireflies
she came alive
her glistening green eyes
bright in the music's ethereal fire

character is the real currency of the realm

dreamer who dreams
while awake
master of the game
you've walked
many times
and lived many lives
tell me, did you think
you knew
what each heartbreak
would feel like?
but you did know
the feeling of
healing yourself
your own warmth stoking
the flames in your heart
until you burn once again
brighter than you ever did before

labour of my love
a castle of stories
built from the wisdom
in my heart
unbreakable,
but in this case
you can draw blood
from the stones

she whispered
in night's breath
I'm going to build
an empire from my heart
a fortress of all that I am
and all the stories in my soul
will live in the star filled sky
in the kingdom in my heart

nothing compares
to the intimate fire inside
after all this time
you can travel everywhere
and experience everything
but what matters most
is the spark you hold
in your heart
and the beauty you carry
in being authentically you

It's myself in the night calling out my name

midnight thoughts
spark the revolution
in my mind
the desire to dream
to be all of me
to feast on the fire
of that electric light
to shine with the stars
of a different kind

like a spark
in the cosmos
of my mind
in the music
it grew
caught fire
and then I
could feel it
all around me
in everything,
in us all
dancing in the waves
of fire and existence
pure ethereal energy
bright and alive
and pulsing
like a heartbeat
me and my
mysterious mind
and the absolute
beauty of it all

she's always enjoyed tapping in
to her own well of power

it takes someone who's been through the dark
and emerged stronger, to know another tortured soul
it's unmistakeable by the smell of their mind
and the sound of their soul music
the colours that radiate from their heart
they've got something different running
through their veins now

you recognise in him
the same spark of light
you know in yourself
and I might say
in those moments
your eyes become
sparkly with tears
your heart beats
on wings of gold,
and the energy of
your soul,
electric

I went in search of treasure
that was already in my heart

I bring the fire in the sky
I cherish the starlight inside me
I shoot to the stars
and the stars fall
like golden lights
into my mind
and onto my tongue
and that's how I'm
the maestro of storytelling

a girl wandering at night around the festivals
she knows her way to slip through quietly
no one sees as she touches the music's essence
and feels the vibrations of the sounds light
no one sees as she jumps across streams
and laughs with the spirits of the water
no one sees as she smiles to the trees
and listens to the melodies from the roots to the leaves
and whispers fairy's wings
no one knows her destiny
a wanderer of magic and stories
with her imagination as the start of it all
a never-ending journey,
with all her heart entwined
the girl who walks the world
of nature's playground
and dreams of stars
no one knows the stories she carries
no one, but her stars

imagination pours into her light
and she drinks from the golden stream
of ideas and magical tidings

all that you've
gone through
in your life
has shaped
the stars
in your heart
and after it all
the real prize
is who you have become

he wasn't my home
I'm my home
and my stories
are what keep
the fire burning
in the fire place

come into the night world
your stories are waiting for you

the thunder in her heart
beats in time with the
rhythm of the universe

she's starting to know
the power of her
own transformation
she bandaged
invisible wounds
with her self-love
in the night's reverie
and realised the
sparkling lights
in who she
is becoming

into the woods we go
to lose ourselves
and find our souls
just follow the sound
of the electronic music

the story written on her skin
she'd made herself into an artist
with every drop of life she has inside
illustrations of colour painted with ink
of course, she's a writer, a storyteller
and so she embodies all that she is
her blood and ink dancing together
in a song, in a story, in her soul

I can feel it
what's mine is mine
like a thousand sparkling
silver shimmers
igniting the air
around my breath
and seeping into my bones

she said walk down by the river
if you're feeling unsure
you'll find what you're looking for
and at dusk I left and told not a soul
and I journeyed over the meadows
down to the river
and found that I did find
what I was looking for
in the reflection in the water under starlight
I saw a girl staring back at me, myself
silent skies with me and my starlight heart
and electric soul

you could always find her
out in the wilderness
soaked in mystery and ancient wisdom
she's dancing with the heartbeat of the world
and nature watches her, watches her wild beauty
and she knows, she is home

she is the lightning wielder
with electricity in her veins

she writes with the colours of her soul

and I realised in
the early hours
of night's embrace
I am my own
eternal cosmos
my imagination
the sail in the wind
I'm dancing to
my own rhythm,
creating melodies of mine
I forged myself in the
embers of the night
I am what I made me

I stared into my turquoise fire
I'd created in the night of magic
I'm beginning to know intimately
the hum of my beating heart

she's always most herself
in the resonance of the light of her soul
matched with the frequency of electricity
she's most alive in her true authenticity

she's midnight poetry
glowing in starlight
ethereal beauty

people wear their secrets on their faces,
look closely and you'll see the deeds they've done

stories unfold in the night time
worlds of imagination and potential
glow with words from her lips
the most precious nights

come dusk,
ghosts of fire
smile at me
in my mind

she's got a golden mind
as sharp as a sword
she's filled it with everything
she's learned
because she knows
a woman's most powerful weapon
is her mind

she dances in her sparkly imagination
tasting of her sweet concoctions
a mind full of vivid illustration
her thoughts never forgotten

I was holding my own hand
walking into mirror dreams
how could I ever know
which reflection was real
if it weren't for the spark in my heart
that refused to burn out

she flies with wings of starlight
onto silver linings
and rests on dreamers' clouds
soft and eternal
as she kisses the night

painted faces, gold stars
become who you really are

now I know the dark night of the soul
here I am, welcome to the world now
welcome to the me I've become

the legend begins here
you decide the story
paint with the
infinite potential
a myth in your mind
made true by you
by your heart
by what you do
and by your
electric soul

and we'll ride on wild horses
into the dark of night
and we leave the hurt behind
and we won't look back
at the path of sorrow
we set on fire
now we choose
to turn the pain into power

the nectar in your kiss
was filled with words
you haven't said

dancing with stardust and encased in dreams
colours of desire in my haunted memories

when the kisses in my heart
sing for more life
and the very fabric
of my being
dances with the sky
I know the story
inside me
is unravelling
into beautiful chaos

she always knew she had stories to write
they were already woven into her soul

in the stars embrace, I am home

there's beautiful braveness brewing in her soul

the falling stars
are flying into hearts
that hold courage to be true

from the sand fairy of Arabian nights
a girl who wanders under candlelight
but when the winds of change howl
and all that you thought you knew
two hearts shattered and broken
when forever is cut
and you bleed from your soul
at the thought of never seeing
his face again
when you're all you have left
you're not a girl anymore
and you find out
what kind of woman you really are

sweet smoky flames
rise up into the air
like her life, she's adapted
to not breathe in the smoke
but breathe in the fire

she drinks deep of the mysteries in her mind
so how could it not be in her nature to be mysterious

electronic music rejuvenates my soul
close my eyes and stand by the speakers
as they beat with my heart
absorbed in the euphoric state
of feeling the sound waves pulsate
and I think this moment will last forever

pioneers whispered to me
in the beckoning dreams
left unanswered
the deepest inspiration
is in finding yourself
all over again

darling, don't ever give up your state of mind

a party of poetry
and whoever makes
the room silent in awe
wins a bottle of witty words
and slick-tongue sentences
though I bet they'd have
their own in abundance

the fire and melodic euphoria in a sea of stars
the nights spent with you kissing our scars
a love that burned and burned
until the flames left new marks
if the price of your choice is yourself
then the cost is too high

electric lights
turn my mind into paradise
I'm as different as they come
playing the beat of my drum
a dream of music glimmers alive
when you think it's lost, the soul survives
learning to play that song again
seek inside when it's all in your head

your stories come alive
in the abyss in your eyes
what did you say to me that night?
a whisper, do or die
your love was a gift and a curse
I'll always belong to myself first

so what are all my writings worth
if I don't live the whole life that I write about
so what if I write about a girl
if I don't become all that I can be

enter the realm
of the soul
here be thyself

electrically charged
every artery and vein
as my blood raced
through my body
and we lit up the night
with electric lights

she runs with the electric energy

it's like my stories came alive
and there's no better feeling
than my imagination dancing
with reality in the ether
thoughts becoming real
and knowing you created
your own world from the dust

midnight carnival in the woods
under starlight's music
witness the marvels of the world
music, magic, mystery
and each night I return
with another story to tell
until the stars run out

summer always had her ways
of bringing new hearts together
in her ripe, fiery glow
and making bonds last
if only for those
long hot, forever romantic nights

meet me in the midnight garden of dreams
forgotten stars live forever here

and once again
I find myself
alone at night
whispering my stories
to the stars
lonely but not lonely
alone and alive
and darling I walk
in the reflection
of that little girl I once was
what if I have always had
all the love I need

write me a poem from your essence
and let me glimpse even the
deepest wounds in your heart
I'll show you my hurt
if you show me yours

it's me in the eye of the storm
I am creation and I am destruction
a butterfly must first go into herself
and transform everything
before she has the wings to fly

some experiences leave a print on us
like a scar on our souls
sometimes a look between two strangers
can tell you all you need to know
and sometimes those strangers become lovers
because you understand that the scar
on their soul is the same as the one on yours

she's left a piece of her heart
somewhere only she would ever know
she wouldn't tell another living soul
she knows she'll never lose herself
because there's a hidden part of her heart
a mysterious part
that's wrapped in stardust
in a place only she knows

she let the words pour
into stranger's hearts
as her lips bled with starlight
leaking from beneath her skin
and with each breath and note
she ripped her scars apart
under those bleeding stars

dive into the electric waves in my imagination
maybe the instruments I choose to play
tune into the waves in my mind

she watched the carnival's converge
in the rainy stained streets
carts carrying crystals and gem stones
fortune tellers shuffling cards
will it be lovers or will it be the temptress
acrobats covered head to toe in tattoos
the carousal churning some enticing lullaby
gold medallions and rings peered from beneath
the boho travellers outfits
like each contained a secret, a memory
it's like they could hear a different song
a strange, magical kind of music
and I was drawn to those
who dared to be different

patterns of paint artistically
signatured on her skin
imprints of stars on her heart
a canvas so beautifully imperfect
it was unquestionably clear
that she had truly lived

how many secrets have
dropped from my lips
as I've told stories to
the owl with amber eyes
lost in night's river
and sailing alone
in the sea of stars
you're the friend
that will anchor with me
in the deep,
wake me up
when I drift to sleep,
always with
your amber eyes

the music and the stories,
if everything else falls away to dust
I know that was real
I know that was true

she lit the lamps with her endless fire
and they burned with her everlasting desire

she smelt like something
I'd never smelt before
like wild berries
and embers syrups
and infinite dreams

catch lightning and change something inside
after heartbreak, survive, then thrive
and then you plunge, and then you rise

I re-live the night we met in my dreams
I was drowning in my sorrows
drinking poison just to soothe the pain
losing myself in the music that night
so I didn't have to hear my own thoughts
dancing in euphoric ecstasy
escaping my life
because I was too afraid to face myself
and then I saw you, sitting there
and I knew, my soul knew
I'd never felt such a visceral reaction
the soul flame that burned in me, burned in you
you were like a lighthouse that I had lit
the fire in centuries ago
my twin flame
I have known you before
whatever happens, however much love
and pain, and hurt, and heartbreak between us
I know I was meant to meet you that night under the
stars
and I'm glad I did
the only word that comes to mind when I think
of you and that night we met
electric

I'm a writer, a poet, a storyteller
I knew it the moment I was old enough
to remember the thoughts inside my head

I write wondrous tales
because the worlds inside my head
make more sense to me than this one
are more real than this one
the trick is making them come true

the ocean waves
are music too
come sunset
and the electricity
in the water
is surging into life
so surf the waves

golden breath stars
that breathe life,
she sings her song
and her music is
a lightning strike
to ignite the fire
with the anthem
never lose the spark
that makes you
you

do you know the colour
of your soul?
if you could imagine it
and paint a picture in
your mind
I have died a thousand times
and brought myself back to life
so now, truth be told
I know the colour of my soul

leaving a trail of stardust and stories
and electricity

no one's ever going to do it like you

she runs wild with her stories
as her words come to life
with the blazing stars

the feeling of knowing
and coming back to oneself
it's like the friend inside the stars

a feeling of gold,
she has it
she knows it now
and her world
becomes limitless

I wrote it in a song darling
all my secrets are there

some people feel the fire
others just feel the burn

the wind of the universe
whistles a tune to me
I want to drink from
the essence of life's ambrosia,
firecrackers explode under
the star-studded sky
burn like the world is
crashing down around you
and you have the flame
that set your soul alight

can you hear the song
of your soul
your music
that rests in you
and plays louder
when you're most alive
it never stops
though at times, it's been so quiet
I almost couldn't hear it
but then when I step into myself again
it's the only thing I hear
so I know the song of my soul

I'll dream of you tonight
when the night brings in the fireflies
gently rest my head
and dream of a love that never dies

and when the summer days
merge into one big chaotic memory
of warm laughter and recklessness
every night, I'd follow her
out to the lake and watch her
stare at the sky in the fading glow
and I'd wonder what she thought
in those moments
because whatever it was
she knew something about the
mystical music of this world
she heard it, it was in her soul
when the day came to an end
and we all sip on delightful things
she hears the soul music of the world
and she dances to it

her mind is bursting with electricity
she hears the spark of the universe
at night she lies awake
and hears synths on
the energy of the world

you're the only drug that could kill me
when you break my heart
dancing with you in the dark
play that song, the one you say
reminds you of me
because at least I know
there, I'll live for eternity

follow the electric lights
thought you were by my side
now in the music I reside
with the spark in my eye
kissing myself back to life

you're creating the music
you need to feed the fire in your heart
and how can I describe the feeling to
someone who has never tasted the stars

success in your veins, you smell of it

only you can fill your own heart

electric soul, starlight heart

tonight I'll kiss the stars
in his heart
with stardust dripping
from my lips
tastes of home
being in his arms
felt like the warmest hug
for my soul

she danced to the midnight music
she keeps in her soul

maybe the heartbreak was meant
to re-ignite the embers
and bring back the flutter of stars
in your eyes,
remember who you are

she's got a glowing solar plexus
life energy,
she's overflowing with it

tell me a story midnight wanderer
one that you whisper to your stars

all those stories that filled your head
let them be alive again

I feel at home when the night comes
and the stars shine in my soul

music festivals will always hold
a deep place in my heart

sugared lips
sweet girl
I had the taste of raspberry cake
and romance in my mouth
are you more Earth
or are you more stars
I've tasted of both
love and loss
with the ferociousness of a
flying arrow
and both hit me
where I needed to be stronger

and even if all the other lights
go out in your heart
in everyone's heart
you'll still find her dancing
under those eternal stars
with a spark in her eye

maybe the only way to
travel to the realm of your heart
is by candlelight in the witching hour
where all spirits of the world linger
to see who will make it out alive

without the stories, life would be dull
but with them, it's bright

put the story in a song with your electronic music
so I can dance and remember our love

sometimes I need to wander off
into a pond of starlight on my own
and tell stories to the stars at midnight
until I feel like me again

I could feel the electricity
pulsing in her veins
and she moved
like lightning strikes
scorching the ground
she danced upon
if any magic exists,
surely she is full of it

my thoughts in my mind
talk to myself pretty
talk to myself kind
courage and confidence
imagination my old friend
stay young forever
story never ends
dance with my creativity
enjoy the festivities
get back up after the fall
it's my story after all

sunrise signals another trail to blaze
for I have not battled with my dragon
in the depths of my unconscious mind
to give up now

the electronic music feeds my soul

to be rare, to be yourself is a heavy toll
that's the price to pay for an electric soul

the real dream catchers
don't chase dreams
they transform themselves
into the person
who already has them

when the storm thundered down
and we gathered in the great hall
by the fireplace
I had never seen the fire so ferocious
perhaps he too knew of the stories
we told as we gazed into his light

inking myself with poems
a permanent message of love

she believes something
chemical happens
when you dance
to the electronic music
ecstasy in your mind
a state of conscious trance
a feeling of ultimate life

and she wrote with her pen
dipped in stolen ink
and drank of
midnight's potion

deep in the woods
the music played
lasers and dragonflies
lights and heartbeats
this is home

star kissed skies
electric vibes
I gave you my heart that night
and I loved you at first sight
never had to swallow
such a hard pill
a part of me knows
I love you and always will

unspoken words
we lay there on a bed
of soft fairy dust
in each other's arms
listening to the music
on and on
we didn't have to say it
but we both knew
our souls danced too

that song had been following me for a while
and that night when I met him for the first time
the same song played in my mind
and I knew why

you let the music say it all
and by the look in your eyes
and the melody of the symphony
I understood, more than you know

music pulsing energy into my soul
I can feel the curious power of it all

I'm made for running wild in the fairy deserts
with the blazing sun piercing my soul
and when dusk arrives and I drink from
the starlight stream
it is those eternal lights
that hear the poetry I keep in my soul
and I hear theirs
a child of the universe you once called me
now a woman with an electric mind
but I have not forgotten the little girl
with a head full of stories
and a heart full of magic
and I see both when I gaze into
those starry waters and see
the reflection of my soul

she's the temptress
draped in stories and tales
poetry falling from her lips
like stars, glowing in the darkness

she's a swirling vortex of sparkling lightning in a bottle
she hears the mind's conversation with the universe

he changed her life in every way
just when she thought
no one heard the music of the stars
he came along

come into the night
who are you really

I'm not who you think I am
stardust runs through my veins
and my heart beats
to the music of the stars

you made me feel so alive
my electricity and your electricity
created the brightest sparks
I'd ever felt
so no matter what
thank you

I'll tell you a story
if you play me a song

because it's in the human heart
where stories really live
not in your books

she's a mixture of beautiful chaos and poetry
in her own world of songs and art
mysterious thoughts in her mind
dancing to an invisible melody
she smiles with her intentions
she'll throw her head back
and howl to the stars
in those moments
I knew by the gleam in her eyes
she's here to live by the rare beat
of her rare heart

musical mind
light me up inside

a walk into desire's eternal realm
enter with electricity in your heart
and your dreams dripping like honey
from your alluring lips
tell me the thoughts
that haunt your mind
the faces dancing in the
darkness of your soul
I can feel your glowing essence
like embers on my skin
maybe I'll tell you a story
or perhaps you are the story
all I know
is that the crossing of our paths
tonight under these stars
started with desire, electricity and dreams

ghost of your song in my lungs

the spark of electricity
that makes us who we are

you can't contain that electric fire
even if you wanted to
and you don't want to
you want to revel in your beauty
all the eternal pleasure it brings you
your mind is too wild to be caged
and your soul is what I see
in those neon lights in your eyes
under the sky at half past three

you're going to paint this city
with the gold dust in your soul
and you know it

soak in the gold dust
as it burns this love
into my heart

your sunlight eyes shone like liquid gold
and you left your light in my soul

our kisses lit up the sky
all electricity awakens
I can't go back to who
I used to be now
change is inevitable
but I feel my feelings
for you will stay with me

music flowing from her lungs
the frequency of fire and love
entangling their magic
until the world caught on fire

music in the vastness
of starlight
echoes in my heart
like a drum of dreams

heartbreak illuminated all the
parts of myself I had forgotten
now I kiss myself goodnight
and every moment remember
the torch that I hold in my heart
is mine to hold only

and you'll watch in wonder
about the girl who became a woman
who paints the stars in her eyes
any colour she chooses

the artistic temperament
she has,
enchanting and unlike
any before her

a voice message from the ether
my tears began flowing because
I knew the sound before he played it
and I felt a kiss on my shoulder
but there was no one there
and the voice whispered
"don't let your heart die"

under the sunset sky
music singing
laughter flowing
stars glowing
under the heart journals in the sky
I lost myself and trusted with all I am
the beat of my heart
and the pulse of my electric soul

she's made of electronic music

and if a look can tell you everything
I knew by the glistening in her eyes
the fire in her soul was coming out tonight

she saw the madness sparkling in his eyes and knew

I'm high on the music and you tonight

she'd walked across the sands of time
swam through starlit seas
danced with lightning in stormy skies
all for a destiny
she'd created at the birth of the cosmos
to be in persistent pursuit
of her greatest potential
and she'd only just begun

lonely nights
dreaming of paradise
a mind like hers
a gift and a curse
a lonely road
far to go

she is dripping
in the amethyst
cosmos magic
from the soles
of her feet
to her breasts
to the electricity
shimmering on her
raspberry blossom lips

what else do I have to say to your heart
that the look in my eyes can't tell you

if it fades away in reality
mix it with fantasy
and who's to say
your imagination
isn't as real as life

light the match
and the stars in your eyes
were more than enough
to warm that ember inside me

stars trickle down my face
the eternal outcasts
have the most life inside
remember the desire for wonder
the lust for life
the fire you had
remember the whispers of
your own heart
before the world
had its way with you
do not lose your spark
do not lose who you are
instead be true always
to your story

and the stars aligned with the ones in her heart

the only one with the power to destroy her light is herself

our hearts were so entangled
together along the journey
if fate labels him a villain,
then so am I

in the cosmic dust
you know the night
is where I keep
my secrets

we were both drunk on stars that night
and you leaned on the desert's hue
and said with utter conviction and sincerity
'I want to taste your tears
see the spark in your heart
sing with the music in your soul
laugh with the darkness and gold
show me all the dreams and the fire
show me how alive you are'

maybe I loved you as soon as I saw you
because in this world of illusionary dust
and half kept promises
I sensed the strength of your beating heart
and there's no force in this world
that could draw me away

when it comes down to it
all I need to know is if your
soul is smiling
when mine is smiling

only when I'm dripping in the essence
of life's mystery
a soul flare in embers
will I swim in the starry stream
of this paradox painting in the sky

I am an endless vortex of
authenticity and imagination
ideas are better than drugs
when you make them real
I could live forever
off the feeling
the natural high

and every serendipitous moment
is like the stars are rippling
in an electric hue
that courses through my own blood
and every time, I smile
in sweet knowing

her body was painted in imagination and mischief
all she could think about was how to paint the stars

come on girl, you're a real one

a song as brutal as it is beautiful
in lyrics and melody
truth not coated in sprinkles
but in piercing light

it started off small
like a seed
like dust on the wind
like a speck in the cosmos
of my mind
a spark
and then in the music it grew
and it caught fire
and then I could feel it all around me
in everything
dancing in the waves of existence
pure ethereal energy

being a writer,
I find being alone
is better to hear
the voices inside my head
and tell the stories
by the fire
that burns eternally within

by every stroke and chord on the violin
the sound waves ripple
in the midnight orchestra
pulsing through the sparkling night
a perfect symphony unfolding
before us
as we danced and dreamed
and drank from the elixir
that music gives to us

because the midnight hour
belongs to loners
writing in alleyways
lovers grabbing each spark
in their shining hearts
misfits playing songs
and the broken one's
coming back to life
in the re-discovery
of the myth of themselves

I'll always love sitting alone at midnight
with wild thoughts, always be that way
that kind of magic is in my DNA

everything is colourful
like an orgasm of power
she exploded across the night sky
she will always be the most beautiful firework

her fingers reached out to
touch those sound waves
electric waves all around her
she played them like a piano
like a musician
and as she moved in dance
she pulled the energy all around her
and it lit up like paintings, like stories
as the music played on
so did the memories become brighter
and the electricity more powerful
until it all encompasses her body
like the lightning inside her

I'm a writer in
the same way
the stars kiss my heart
I make sense of the world
as I twirl in words
of creation and imagination
endlessly reinventing myself
a story, a plot twist
beauty in a heartfelt story
the only one who needs to feel
the truth in the voices I bring to life
is me

and maybe our stories,
their faces
your legends
will endure endless time
it will certainly be alive forever
in the hearts of all those rebels

a walk over curiosity's eternal waterfall
skies of stars and celestial light
I need not hear any song
but the one I'm composing
for my life journey
in the depths of my heart

what do we know more intimately
than the inner turmoil's of our hearts

the night is an escape into the
wonder of it all
and in the night we fly
and in the night we're king

rare breed
maybe you're the last of us

euphoria under the night sky
those twinkling stars never die
electricity ignites in the air inside our lungs
the night is always young
with every beat and melody
lightning strikes with that neon sky
play it again, singer of the night
dance together, the dark and the light
in the music we never grow old
alive in the sound, with electric souls

walk through the fire
with every elegance
you possess
with your notorious soul

and when the ashes of youth
blow in the southern wind
and we tie up loose ends
of lovers and burnt out flames
what do we have left
but the pain and the euphoria

some thoughts are like cherry sweets
they just taste good in my mind

then he played his electric music
and I listened
and I understood completely
and it felt like no words
could describe it better
than that music could

get back up again
come back with
even more dazzling
stars in your veins
even more fire
in your eyes
and take back
what you know is
yours all along

maybe no one will ever be
able to understand how deep
your river flows
or know the taste of the honey
that drips from your lips
onto the stars
as you tell your stories
maybe that is for you
and you alone

she always knew
to write her story
she'd have to be alone
just her and her stars
and the thought of
forever in the air
now and again
she'd disappear for a while
to write parts of her story

she danced under the stars
the stars watched her
and she knew it

alone in dreams
your heart whispers
only words you know
for you, it boom booms
to that lightning
in your mind
more and more
you play
on that harmonious
synchronicity
like a piano of emotion
now you feel the transformation
start to glow in your veins
and you know you're going to
burn with a different light

I thought you were forever
and now, my stories are all I have left

what good are stories with no one to tell them to

are you afraid little girl?
afraid of the thoughts you might think
if you listen to yourself at night
instead of drowning in an ecstasy filled cocoon
filled with music and excess,
will you ever fill the void?
are you afraid of what you've had to become
before you can transform into the butterfly
it's you, you have forever
you thought you had to live that way
but now the world is yours
and it always has been and always will be
so find your courage once again
and live your life
with your electric soul

everything came alive
in the electricity
of her soul

Elise x

Printed in Great Britain
by Amazon